This book is dedicated to the many who
have helped us help others. We
couldn't have done it without you.

Introduction:

Its 7 am during a holiday break from school. The house is quiet and everyone, including the dog, is still sleeping. Wait- what is that glow coming from downstairs? Oh yeah, now I remember it's Nick "playing" (and I use this term to its broadest meaning) with his friends. This is the new generation of social media and gamers. Gone are the days of riding your bike until dark or playing whiffle ball at the park until someone hits the ball so far it gets run over by a car and then the game is over. "Why go out and play risking skin cancer," is the most convenient reply Nick quips, "when I can play with my friends inside?" This involves sitting in front of the ever-glowing television with headsets that will later be responsible for hearing loss in his thirties, and screaming at his friends "shoot, shoot, behind you ..."

What can I do as a parent? How can I send him outside to play when all the other kids are glued to their phones, iPad, gamer sets? What to do?

Nick and I decide, let's have them all come over and socially ignore each other together, while eating snacks and texting. Great idea I say, thinking that once they are all together someone will suggest they play something that requires dialogue.

Word gets out of the new plan and seven kids find their way to our house. Mostly girls, with one other boy and Nick, and what happens is nothing short of a miracle. They want to play charades. Kids are talking and laughing and all it takes is a small investment of capital for pizza, soda and junk food.

This goes on for a few hours, until someone takes a picture to post on a social media site, then phones are whipped out and the TV goes on. Ugh! We were on to something.

"Let's try again next month," I say as I drive each kid home. All agree for a repeat of fun.

Here's where the Voluntweens of Drexel Hill begin. Before the next meeting, Nick and I create a plan of attack, play a little, then suggest the idea of this volunteer group. The kids that had come over last month are some of the brightest and sensible youngsters in his elementary school. They come from families that are involved in school activities, but most importantly they are involved in their kids' lives and are just wonderful parents. Nick explains the idea of the group and that everyone will have a job to do, a responsibility, with fun and food to be included.

We are now officially the Voluntweens of Drexel Hill, as both an Instagram page and Facebook group are created (finally a constructive reason for the kids to get on their phones).

The word is out....

More kids shown an interest in the group and want to join because we're now on social media and the more photos or quotes posted, the more "likes" are generated, and what kid doesn't want to be part of that?

Even with three rows of seating in my car and my husband now involved, we can't transport more than 11 kids to each outing/service event. How can I turn away kids who want to help make the community better? Feelings get hurt as some are told we are operating at full capacity, but at the same time we also suggest that their parents begin an initiative of their own.

Our final count, as of now, is 4 boys and 8 girls – yes that equals 12, as one kid rides on the roof (LOL- see I can be a fun mom too).

Over the next few months this group of pre-teens plan and execute with great success fundraising, volunteering and donating to not only the local community but also nationally. They are recognized with awards from their beloved elementary school, as well as winning gift cards from local department stores for their community services and money donations contributed by local businesses to help further their goals. Beneficiaries of their efforts send "Thank You" cards by way of the US Postal Service.

Teachers at school hear the chatter of the Voluntweens and ask how they can help. One entire 5th grade class helps write and decorate Valentines for Vets, which we deliver with candy to the Philadelphia Veterans Hospital. This is fun, this is fulfilling, and this is volunteering with maximum hands on social activity.

Looking forward to the close of 2013, we have many more activities planned: a walk-a-thon that will collect money for cancer research that is donated to the local children's' hospital, a Voluntweens-made and served dinner for our local volunteer fire department – where we will use the money we raised at our baseball game to buy the food, and much more.

The rest of this book consists of stories and pictures of the Voluntweens members and their achievements thus far, in their own words, and ideas for your own pre-teen/teen to start a group of their own. At the end, you will find a list of resources to help your new group develop.

The original members of the Voluntweens at one of their first meetings. All the baby items and personal hygiene products behind them, purchased with coupons and donated gift cards, were delivered to a women's shelter for mothers and babies. The Voluntweens collected coupons from their friends, neighbors and teachers, then scoured advertising flyers and planned their strategy. They went to the local supermarket, competitively shopped and saved.

Members from left to right: Joseph, Nickolas, Sara, Meryn, Alyssa, Colleen, Chloe.

The current Voluntweens June 2013 partnered with the Camden Riversharks baseball team for a fundraiser. Throughout a rain-delayed contest, the kids had fun as they raised $250.00, which may be small to some, but was a success in their eyes!

The Voluntweens held a book drive in April with the help of their principal and teachers at Hillcrest Elementary. Over the course of two weeks they collected more than 550 gently-used books that they then organized, packed, and shipped to incarcerated mothers throughout the country that they could then read to their kids on vistiting days.

It took the Voluntweens over 3 hours to sort and package over 15 boxes of books before heading to the post office.

Scrapbook

As the Voluntweens grew in membership, they were presented with the Character Counts

Award for Caring in 2013 by Principal Chris Pugliese of Hillcrest Elementary, for the book drive

that became an overwhelming success.

Members from left to right- Nick, Joe, Sara, Alyssa, Colleen, Emma, Chloe, Meryn and Gavin.

Hi, my name is Nickolas Moncilovich and I am 11 years old. I just finished 5th grade at Hillcrest

Elementary school in Drexel Hill, Pa. The above picture is from our February project where our challenge was to buy as much pet food we could using coupons that were donated from our neighbors and friends, spending only $10.00. We donated all this food to our local SPCA.

Our group, the Voluntweens, likes to help others, as well as animals. I personally like to help other people, make them feel happy and secure just like anyone else. We have collected food, clothes, books and other items that help those that need it.

As a pre-teen or teenager yourself, you can help your community using no money by just cleaning up littered areas once a month. There are so many people that can benefit by forming a group with your friends. We have helped the homeless vets, hurricane victims, school children and even inmates throughout the country. I always think about what I would do if I won a lot of money; my answer is give half for donations to charity groups and put the other half away for college.

When I graduate high school in 2020, I plan to attend college to study law, and also play college baseball, which is my favorite activity to participate in. If you want, you can follow my activities on Instagram at nick_mono7.

Hi I'm Joe Ricci. Before the Voluntweens I did volunteer work for my brother's charity Tommy's gifts for Kids (...http://www.tommysgiftsforkids.com/....) and I still do. We give toys to kids who have cancer at DuPont Children's hospital.

Whenever a kid gets a toy, teddy bear or a doll, they have a great big smile and that makes you feel great.

One day my friend Nick came up to me and gave me a letter that said, "You have been invited to be in the Voluntweens of Drexel Hill." I didn't know what the Voluntweens were so I kept reading and then I understood. The Voluntweens are a group of pre-teens that do charity work for lots of people. So I joined and I'm happy I did. We do charity work but we also have a lot of fun.

To me, the Voluntweens show that just because you are young, it doesn't mean you can't put down your electronics and make a difference. We have bought food for the homeless shelter twice, we've been the dream team at the Camden Riversharks game, and raised over $250.00 and held a book drive at our school. The Voluntweens have accomplished a lot.

I never thought that I would be this involved with charity work, but I'm glad I am. We've accomplished so much so far and it's only going to get better. So remember, if you're a pre-teen -- put down your electronics and go out and help. If you're a teenager or older, what are you doing reading this? Go out and do some charity work. Maybe you could even start your own group of volunteers, and who knows, you could end up making a big difference in your area. You can start out small, but you'll grow to do bigger and better things.

Hi, my name is Della George. I just finished school at Hillcrest Elementary and I am going to Drexel Hill Middle School in the fall for sixth grade. My favorite activities besides the Voluntweens are mostly having fun with my family and friends. I also love sports. I play field hockey, basketball and softball. I like helping others because it's a nice thing to do. Just think about how your parents help you, without them you would be lost. Even though I'm not as experienced as my parents, I still like helping others in need. I think any average kid trying to help others can do even simple things like picking up trash when they see it, rather than just walking by. I would encourage all pre-teens to start a group like ours. Often just talking to people and trying to help them figure out their problems can help.

The people who I think need the most help are people who don't have anyone to love and support them. When you have no one life is hard.

If I had a million dollars, to be honest, I would keep some and use some to help others.

When I graduate from high school, I want to go to Neumann College and get a job as a nurse or police officer. The Voluntweens is a very fun group. I think more people should start making groups like ours.

Hi, my name is Alyssa Oreskovich. I go to school at Drexel Hill Middle School. My favorite

activities besides volunteering are playing softball, field hockey, basketball, hockey, and riding

my bike!! I started volunteering when I was in third grade. I was in a group that helped moms

with kids who were homeless. Then two years later I joined the Voluntweens when the group first started. I like to help others because some people need more that I do. For example, when I was in third grade we donated things for the moms and their children. Now in fifth grade I do book drives , go shopping at the supermarket and get stuff for the Marines, homeless people and for the moms who are in need. An average kid can help others by starting a group to help others. Helping someone cross the street, or kids can prepare a meal to bring to the homeless shelter. They can also have a fundraiser to help raise money for people who need it. One activity I would like to do is collect toys for children who don't have any, and then personally drop them off to the children. I think homeless people need more help because they don't have anything. We have food, shelter, and clothing and they don't. We could help them by giving them some of our gently used clothes and extra food. We can shelter them by showing them where local churches and organizations are that will provide a warm or cool place for them to sleep.

If I had a million dollars I would give some of it to different charities and I would use the rest to pay for college. When I graduate from high school, I would like to become a veterinarian because I want to help animals.

If you are interested in helping others in your community, you can create your own volunteer group with several of your friends. Every community has a need for volunteers.

My name is Sara Sullivan, I just finished 5th grade at Hillcrest Elementary and now I am going to go to Drexel Hill Middle School. My favorite activities to do besides volunteering are softball, field hockey, basketball and hanging out with friends. I got started volunteering by doing Girl Scouts. We made blankets for a homeless shelter, we made PB & J sandwiches for a food bank. We also collected canned goods at Thanksgiving for a homeless shelter. Myself and some friend in the group also collected money at school for Hurricane Sandy Relief.

I like to help others because it gives me a warm feeling inside that I did something right. I also enjoy helping people because I am a caring person. An average kid can help others by donating food to a local food bank, or just helping a neighbor with groceries. It doesn't have to be a big deal, it can be little as long as you help out. One activity that I would like to do to help others is to go to a children's' ward at a hospital and visit with them, play and read a book to them. Even do crafts or just sit and talk to them.

My name is Chloe Ondria. I am 11 years old and I go to Drexel Hill Middle School. My favorite activities are gymnastics, dancing, lacrosse and cooking. I started helping others when my mom died. She died of cancer when I was 8 years old. The Voluntweens is not the first group I volunteered for. My first charity was called "Friendship for Charity." My friends and I made bracelets and sold them to people passing by. We made $49 and gave it to a hospital so they could use it for cancer research. I also did a charity where my friends and I collected money and donated it to the Red Cross. I like helping others because it makes me feel special, and that I know I am making people smile every day.

An average kid can help others by just sharing something with someone who doesn't have a lot. One activity that I would like to do is to help donate items to children who have cancer. I think that homeless people need help, like a shelter to live in, help with clothing and food. I also think that cancer patients need help because they go through a lot and they need cheering up.

You can follow me and our activities by following me at @chloesbunnies on Instagram.

"One cannot feel self-worth without giving"- Hirshan El Rouby

Hi, my name is Gavin Merrin. I wanted to volunteer and help the Voluntweens because I know there are a lot of people that need help. I think if everyone did a little volunteering, the world would be a better place. Everyone would treat each other kinder too. The first thing we did after I joined was to collect books for mothers in jail that they now have to read to their children when they visit. We even had a fun time doing it together.

Another thing we did was collect coupons in order to save money on groceries. We did this because we wanted to get the most food we could to help families. We learned how to save when we shop at the grocery store and how expensive it can be for families.

We are also going to get together and cook a meal for our volunteer firefighters in our neighborhood.

If I had a million dollars I would give all of it to the Red Cross. After high school I would like to go in to the Marines and serve my country.

My name is Cassidy Elizabeth Behl. I am entering sixth grade at Drexel Hill Middle School. My favorite activities are dancing, reading, swimming and spending time with my family and friends. I started to volunteer with the help of my family and friends and volunteering in other activities through church and school. We would donate clothing and food to the poor and collect items for the victims of Hurricane Sandy. We also collected and sent items for the children and victims of Sandy Hook. Volunteering is a wonderful thing to do because it makes you feel great inside and out. It also makes the person you are helping feel good too. Any kid could help others by cleaning up trash in their neighborhood, go to a nursing home and visit with the elderly, or just sit with a neighbor who has no one to visit them. There are so many things we can do to help in our community. The one activity I would like to do is visit sick children in the hospital. Just to put a smile on their face and maybe read them a book or make crafts.

If I had a million dollars I would try to help as many people as possible. I would like to create an organization to help children who have lost a parent at a young age.

When I graduate high school I would like to go to college to become a teacher. Teachers help us so much in the community. I hope someday I am able to help children like my teachers have helped and cared for me. All kids should go out and volunteer; we can make a difference even if we are just pre-teens. Get your friends together and let's make the world a better place!

My name is Meryn Steinrock. I go to school at Drexel Hill Middle School. My favorite activities besides volunteering are shopping, swimming, basketball, lacrosse, field hockey, softball and hanging out with friends. I like to help others because it's a nice thing to do and makes me feel good when I do it. All kids can help in many ways. They can donate clothes, food, and even their time. Kids can get together in making a group to do charity work. One activity that I would personally like to do is to go to a nursing home and help the elderly with things they may need help with, and bring them flowers and cards.

People that I think need help are the less fortunate than myself and the chidren that have no families. If I had a million dollars I would give half to a charity and the other half to use to pay for college.

When I graduate from high school I want to go to college and become successful. All pre-teens can make a difference by doing something for someone, so go out and make the world a better place.

There are 3 other members of our current group; Evan (below), Colleen and Emma who will be saving their bios for book number 2!

Emma (above) and Colleen (below)

Riversharks fundraiser June 2013......... Voluntweens take the field with the players!

Shopping for Homeless Vets pantry challenge May 2013

Nick, Joe, and Gavin- one of the few times the boys won't argue about food shopping!

Following page shows Colleen and Sara shopping with coupons and then below photo of Nick at

the Vets Home where all the food was delivered on Memorial Day.

July 2013 meeting for discussion of Fireman's dinner and Cancer Walk

RESOURCES FOR STARTING A GROUP OF VOLUNTWEENS IN YOUR AREA

Online sites that are kid friendly, easy to maneuver and straightforward:

Volunteermatch.org

Dosomething.org

Contact local minor league ball clubs in your area. As you read in this book we partnered with the Camden Riversharks of New Jersey, but several states have multiple minor league teams that help with fundraising.

Below is an example of the flyers that the Riversharks provided to us to help advertise our fundraiser:

Check out our Facebook page – Voluntweens of Drexel Hill

<u>Local and national stores that help with fundraising:</u>

Five Below- National stores (www.fivebelow.com) will give 10% of sales back to your group : host a fundraiser with a date during the year when lots of friends and families go to Five Below like 2 weeks before Halloween, 2 weeks before back to school in august.

Menchie's Yogurt (www.menchies.com) - With over 250 stores nationwide and overseas, this make-your-own yogurt cup store is always jammed with kids. They help organize fundraisers and donate part of the total sales for your day right back to your organization.

Pinkberry Yogurt (www.pinkberry.com) - This yogurt store will help you with your fundraiser by providing flyers and donate 20% of sales during your fundraiser back to your organization. *Please note: Pinkberry Fundraisers are only available to non-profit organizations with recognized 501-C3 Federal tax status.*

Tony Roni's Pizza (www.tonyronis.com) - Philadelphia suburb pizza shops that will help plan your fundraiser day and donate 10% of sales back to your organization. Prefect day to pick is a Friday during lent where cheese pizzas are made by the 100's. Who doesn't love pizza?

Krispy Kreme Donuts (www.krispykreme.com) - They have 4 different options to help secure a fundraiser for your group. My favorite is selling their" one dozen donuts certificates". Perfect for those days where you are the snack mom for school activities.

McDonald's fast food restaurants - Depending on your local McDonald's, the fast food chain often will give up to 25% of sales during your fundraiser; however adults must primarily run the fundraiser, by working the registers with the staff, while the pre-teens help clear tables, sweep the floor, stock beverage areas. Once again, almost everyone has eaten at McDonalds.

Five Guys Burgers and Fries (www.fiveguys.com) - National burger stores will also provide you with flyers that have your fundraiser date- Depending on volume of sales during your day, your group will get between 15-25% of the sales. If you've never tried these burgers, it's a must! Over 1000 stores nationwide.

TGIF- Fundraise @ T.G.I. Friday's™ -Simply choose a T.G.I. Friday's® restaurant in your area and invite supporters of your organization to dine at that restaurant on a pre-determined date and time. TGI Friday's Inc. and SRAC Casual Dining, LLC will donate 20% of all pre-tax sales generated by your group back to your non-profit organization.

Sonic Drive In - Your local SONIC DRIVE IN can sponsor a fundraising event where your organization can earn a certain percentage of sales from 5 to 8PM on a predetermined night. This is a great way to bring students, staff and parents together to raise money for your organization.

Chipotle Mexican Grill (www.chipolte.com) - National stores will sponsor in-restaurant fundraisers for your group.

Outback Steakhouse (www.outback.com) - Outback Steakhouse takes great pride in giving back. They have a strong commitment to improve the quality of life in each of our communities. "Being good neighbors is more than just an idea; it is the driving force in how we do business. Each of our restaurants seeks out local groups and events with which to share its food, time and money. By enlisting the volunteer spirit of our Outbackers, our restaurants create awareness of local groups and help build our communities from within."

These are just a small sampling of the businesses that can help your group get started. Make sure to have a plan and be willing to explain what you plan to do with the funds that you raise. Take lots of pictures during your event that you can later share with local papers, or the chain itself. They may promote it on their local website, which in turn promotes your group.